Depression Journal: Daily Check-In

Depression Journal:
Daily Check-In

75 Days of Reflection Space
to Track and Understand
Your Symptoms

Missy Beck, MA, LMFT

ROCKRIDGE
PRESS

For general information on our other products and services or to obtain technical support, please contact our Customer Care Department within the United States at (866) 744-2665, or outside the United States at (510) 253-0500.

Rockridge Press publishes its books in a variety of electronic and print formats. Some content that appears in print may not be available in electronic books, and vice versa.

TRADEMARKS: Rockridge Press and the Rockridge Press logo are trademarks or registered trademarks of Callisto Media Inc. and/or its affiliates, in the United States and other countries, and may not be used without written permission. All other trademarks are the property of their respective owners. Rockridge Press is not associated with any product or vendor mentioned in this book.

Interior and Cover Designer: Scott Petrower
Art Producer: Hannah Dickerson
Production Editor: Dylan Julian
Production Manager: Jose Olivera

All illustrations used under license from Shutterstock.com
Author photo courtesy of Louie Dio

Paperback ISBN: 978-1-63807-688-9
R0

CONTENTS

Introduction vii

PART 1:
Depression and How It Manifests 1

PART 2:
Tracking and Journaling through Depression 7

PART 3:
75 Daily Trackers 15

Resources 167

References 168

INTRODUCTION

Welcome! As a licensed psychotherapist who has been practicing for more than 10 years, I am no stranger to depression. I have worked with countless clients who have struggled to varying degrees with their own depression. What may not be as obvious is that I, too, have had my own battle with depression. There is a false belief that therapists do not have mental health challenges, or that we somehow can rise above them because it is "what we do." The truth is, though therapists are able to hold space for our clients and help them do the work, we also deal with our own mental health struggles and how to navigate them. I have been working on myself, either in my own therapy or through self-help modalities such as journaling, since I was 10 years old. Journaling has created the space for me to be with my own thoughts in a safe and nonjudgmental way. It has also helped me learn to deeply self-reflect and notice patterns and themes in my life. And as a result of these recognitions, I have been able to implement small, incremental changes that have helped me feel less stuck and depressed.

I went through a particularly dark time in my early 20s, and I know how difficult, bleak, and isolating depression can feel. At the time, there were not as many resources available and mental health was not as widely discussed as it is today. This journal provides an opportunity to self-reflect and track where you are in your mental health journey. As you begin to work on this journal, please know how incredibly brave and courageous you are. And remember: Greater happiness is always possible.

PART 1

Depression and How It Manifests

You are not a depressed person but rather a person who is experiencing depression. Being depressed does not define who you are.

Understanding Depression

You are not alone in experiencing depression. Depression is one of the most common mental health conditions affecting the population today. In fact, according to the American Psychiatric Association, one in six people will face depression at some point in their lives. So, what exactly is depression? *Depression* is defined as persistent feelings of sadness, hopelessness, and irritability, along with a lack of interest in and motivation to do usual daily activities.

This can affect how you interact with the world both personally and professionally. However, it is important to note that depression is not one-size-fits-all. It can manifest itself in different ways, impacting your emotional, spiritual, and physical states, thus changing how you think, feel, and even behave. The root causes of depression are multifaceted and can include biological, psychological, and social factors. Difficult life events such as the loss of a loved one, divorce, the inability to work, various health conditions, and trauma can also contribute to depression.

This journal is not intended to be a substitute for professional help. If you are seeing a mental health-care provider, please continue to do so. It is also important to note that if you feel that your depressive symptoms are no longer manageable on your own, you should seek professional help immediately.

Symptoms of Depression

Symptoms of depression vary from person to person and can range from mild to severe. That being said, there are common features that characterize depression—many of which you will track in this journal. Feelings of despair, sadness, and agitation, as well as a lack of interest in and motivation to do the things you used to enjoy doing, are often signs of depression. Other common features include withdrawing socially, isolating yourself, and feeling alone. Self-esteem is often diminished, creating feelings of worthlessness, self-doubt, and low self-confidence. Your ability to concentrate may be thwarted, and making even the smallest decisions can seem impossible.

You may also notice mood and behavioral changes. These can include feelings of anger, aggression, or impulsivity. An increase in anxiety and excessive worry are also common.

Certain people or situations may trigger you in a way they didn't used to.

Physical symptoms can occur, as well. Your appetite can fluctuate, causing you to overeat or undernourish yourself. Some people experience insomnia, while others might sleep for hours on end. Energy levels may decrease and fatigue may increase. Headaches, body aches, and pain are also common. The Daily Tracker worksheets in part 3 will allow you to track your physical symptoms, triggers, and moods so you can begin recognizing patterns in your behavior and thoughts.

In severe cases of depression, one may experience thoughts of suicide or suicidal ideation. If you are experiencing either of these, please reach out for help immediately by calling the National Suicide Prevention Lifeline at 1-800-273-8255 (available 24/7). It is important that you get the medical help and attention you need and do not suffer alone.

Healthy Habits

There's no one way to combat symptoms of depression. Treatment can include the use of psychotherapy, psychotropic medicine, or more holistic approaches such as the use of this journal. Journaling and tracking your emotions and daily activities helps you notice patterns in your thoughts, behaviors, and symptoms. It can be difficult to make changes in our lives when we are unaware of these patterns or how we are showing up (or not showing up) for ourselves. As we track, we start to see how our mood fluctuations, sleep patterns, ability to concentrate, triggers, and energy levels (as well as other physical symptoms) shift from day to day. In addition to tracking, asking self-reflective questions also offers us an opportunity to look within and begin to anticipate as well as plan ways of managing our depression. For example, if you see that your energy levels are particularly low in the morning, plan to get groceries or run errands in the afternoon. Or if you notice that your anxiety is high, use techniques to ground yourself in the present moment (see page 25).

As we become more aware of our patterns and symptoms, we can begin making small, incremental changes that support us in feeling less stuck, isolated, and depressed.

Reflecting on Your Feelings

Most of us were not taught how to sit with uncomfortable emotions. Traditional schooling does not include classes on how to manage our feelings. And as children, we may have been sent to our rooms or asked to take a time-out when the outward expression of our feelings seemed too big or too much for the adults caring for us. Rather than learning how to tolerate these distressing emotions, most of us compensate by repressing them. As adults, this learned behavior can leave us incapable of managing our emotions. Many of us struggle to identify what we are actually feeling—and when we are able to pinpoint the feeling, it usually comes with a hefty dose of judgment.

So how can we be expected to do something that we have never learned to do? The approach is quite simple: time, practice, grace, and self-compassion. When we begin to track our feelings and notice the thoughts and behaviors that follow, we start to become more comfortable in this space. In fact, research shows that with practice, the neuroplasticity of our brains can actually form new pathways, thus creating new ways of being. It is through our ability to sit with these difficult emotions and not repress them that we can learn to accept what we are experiencing without judgment and, ultimately, rewire our brains.

PART 2

Tracking and Journaling through Depression

It can be difficult to see the sunshine through a storm, but remember that the rain does stop, clouds do pass, and, if you look closely, you may even see a rainbow on the other side.

Initial Check-In

When beginning a journaling practice, it is important that you first establish an accurate baseline of what you are feeling. It is difficult to assess how far you have come or what you need to continue working on without knowing where you started. When we are experiencing depression, it's easy to think that we know where we are at, labeling ourselves as depressed without clearly articulating what depression looks like for us. The following questions will help you reflect on and identify the feelings that are coming up and what has triggered those emotions, as well as negative thought patterns and beliefs that keep you stuck. Please be sure to allow yourself the space and time to answer these questions as honestly as possible and create a starting place for your journaling practice.

What adjectives would you use to describe your depression and how you feel? If you're not sure how to describe your feelings, take a look at the list the Hoffman Institute has compiled (see Resources, page 167).

When did these feelings start, and how long have you felt this way?

What negative thought patterns and self-talk can you identify?

Where do you feel your depression in your body?

Do you notice anything specific that triggers your feelings of depression?

What are the top five stressors you believe are causing your depression?

TRACKING AND JOURNALING THROUGH DEPRESSION   9

Is there anything you are currently doing that helps manage your depression?

....

....

Goals

Depression can feel exhausting, hopeless, and never-ending. However, we can start to see a light at the end of the tunnel and a hope for something different when we set goals to help manage our depression. Setting goals allows us to create a desired result for something we are working toward. When you are experiencing depression, it can be difficult to imagine the fog lifting, but as you answer the following questions, you may find that you can envision a future that looks and feels different from your current mental health state. Be sure to set goals that are realistic and involve small, incremental changes. For example, if you struggle to exercise, you can set the goal of going on a walk for 10 minutes each day. Baby steps are small victories!

What adjectives describe how you want to feel in the future?

....

....

What are three small habits you can implement now that can help support you?

....

....

How would you like to feel in your body?

....

....

What can you do now to take care of your body?

....

....

Who in your life helps lift your spirit, and how can you plan to spend more time with them?

....

....

What is one goal you can set that is challenging yet attainable?

Tracking Your Symptoms

In the tracker you will see seven different sections to fill out daily:

Date: Enter the date for each entry. This will allow you to look back and see what you were feeling each day.

Sleep: Record the time you went to sleep, the time you woke up, and the total number of hours you slept each night. You can also note any themes or ideas you remember from your dreams.

Mood/Feelings: Note in each box what your mood was at the start, middle, and end of each day. You can use words, a number scale (1–10), or any other method that allows you to notate your mood.

Triggers: Record the time that you felt triggered, what the trigger was, how you responded, and what emotion you experienced. For example, "A friend didn't text me back, I responded by texting again, and I felt insecure and angry."

Physical Symptoms: Check all the boxes that apply to how you are physically feeling that day. You can also fill in and add any words that are not listed.

Concentration/Focus: Circle the number on the scale that corresponds to your level of concentration/focus that day.

Social Engagement: List who you engaged with and how you felt in their company. If you didn't see anyone and/or preferred to be alone, check that box.

Understanding What You're Writing

When we are depressed, we experience difficult emotions. Most of us want to find a way to suppress or ignore these feelings rather than to sit and feel them. Through journaling and tracking, we can begin identifying patterns in our behaviors, thoughts, and emotions. Journaling helps us slow down, reflect, find clarity, and manage our stress in a safe and healthy way, ultimately teaching us how to sit with all our feelings. Follow these steps to get started:

Make journaling a part of your schedule. It is important to dedicate a specific time in your day to journaling. When we commit to doing something at a set time, we begin to form habits.

Find a quiet space. Try to find a quiet place where you will not be distracted. Consider silencing your phone and setting a timer for 5 to 20 minutes to work on journaling each day.

Do what works for you. Some people find it useful to write paragraphs and others prefer to use bullet points or dash marks. It does not matter what method you use, so long as it works for you.

Write about hard things. As you reflect on your day, notice what may have triggered difficult emotions, how you responded, and how you are feeling now.

Let your thoughts flow. It can be easy to get caught up in our heads and start to censor what we write. This is *your* journal, so allow it to be a place of nonjudgment, authenticity, and vulnerability. Remember, this is for your eyes only!

Create time to reflect on what you wrote. Don't forget to take time to reflect on and sit with the feelings that come up throughout the journaling process. By allowing yourself the space and time to be with your feelings, you are creating new, healthy ways of managing your emotions rather than pushing them away.

75 Daily Trackers

There is no straight path to healing.
Some days feel better than others,
and what truly matters is our ability to
be present with what we are feeling
and experiencing in each moment.

DAILY TRACKER

Today's Date: _____

Went to sleep at: _____ Woke up at: _____ Total hours slept: _____

MOOD / FEELINGS TRACKER			
	Start of Day	Middle of Day	End of Day
Notes			

TRIGGER TRACKER			
Time	Trigger	How did I respond?	What did I feel?

Physical Symptoms:

☐ ENERGIZED	☐ ACHY	☐ RELAXED
☐ TIRED	☐ SLUGGISH	☐ WELL-RESTED
☐ REFRESHED	☐ FATIGUED	☐ JITTERY
☐ WEAK	☐ NUMB	☐ STRONG
☐ _____	☐ _____	☐ _____

Concentration / Focus:

NO ABILITY TO FOCUS   1   2   3   4   5   6   7   8   9   10   VERY FOCUSED

SOCIAL ENGAGEMENT	
Who did I see today?	How did I feel in their company?

☐ I preferred to be alone today

You spend more time talking to yourself than to anyone else. How can you speak to yourself in a kinder way?

DAILY TRACKER

Today's Date: _____

Went to sleep at: _____ Woke up at: _____ Total hours slept: _____

MOOD / FEELINGS TRACKER

	Start of Day	Middle of Day	End of Day
Notes			

TRIGGER TRACKER

Time	Trigger	How did I respond?	What did I feel?

Physical Symptoms:

☐ ENERGIZED	☐ ACHY	☐ RELAXED
☐ TIRED	☐ SLUGGISH	☐ WELL-RESTED
☐ REFRESHED	☐ FATIGUED	☐ JITTERY
☐ WEAK	☐ NUMB	☐ STRONG
☐ _____	☐ _____	☐ _____

Concentration / Focus:

NO ABILITY TO FOCUS 1 2 3 4 5 6 7 8 9 10 VERY FOCUSED

SOCIAL ENGAGEMENT

Who did I see today?	How did I feel in their company?

☐ I preferred to be alone today

What did you most enjoy doing as a child? How can you implement this activity into your present life?

DAILY TRACKER

Today's Date: _____

Went to sleep at: _____ Woke up at: _____ Total hours slept: _____

MOOD / FEELINGS TRACKER			
	Start of Day	Middle of Day	End of Day
Notes			

TRIGGER TRACKER			
Time	Trigger	How did I respond?	What did I feel?

Physical Symptoms:

☐ ENERGIZED ☐ ACHY ☐ RELAXED
☐ TIRED ☐ SLUGGISH ☐ WELL-RESTED
☐ REFRESHED ☐ FATIGUED ☐ JITTERY
☐ WEAK ☐ NUMB ☐ STRONG
☐ _____ ☐ _____ ☐ _____

Concentration / Focus:

NO ABILITY TO FOCUS   1   2   3   4   5   6   7   8   9   10   VERY FOCUSED

SOCIAL ENGAGEMENT	
Who did I see today?	How did I feel in their company?

☐ I preferred to be alone today

What are five words you would ideally like to be described as? Why?

DAILY TRACKER

Today's Date: _____

Went to sleep at: _____ Woke up at: _____ Total hours slept: _____

MOOD / FEELINGS TRACKER			
	Start of Day	Middle of Day	End of Day
Notes			

TRIGGER TRACKER			
Time	Trigger	How did I respond?	What did I feel?

Physical Symptoms:

- ☐ ENERGIZED
- ☐ TIRED
- ☐ REFRESHED
- ☐ WEAK
- ☐ _____

- ☐ ACHY
- ☐ SLUGGISH
- ☐ FATIGUED
- ☐ NUMB
- ☐ _____

- ☐ RELAXED
- ☐ WELL-RESTED
- ☐ JITTERY
- ☐ STRONG
- ☐ _____

Concentration / Focus:

NO ABILITY TO FOCUS 1 2 3 4 5 6 7 8 9 10 VERY FOCUSED

SOCIAL ENGAGEMENT	
Who did I see today?	How did I feel in their company?

☐ I preferred to be alone today

What are three things you are proud of yourself for doing today?
(These can be big or small—even brushing your teeth counts!)

DAILY TRACKER

Today's Date: _____

Went to sleep at: _____ Woke up at: _____ Total hours slept: _____

MOOD / FEELINGS TRACKER			
	Start of Day	Middle of Day	End of Day
Notes			

TRIGGER TRACKER			
Time	Trigger	How did I respond?	What did I feel?

Physical Symptoms:

☐ ENERGIZED	☐ ACHY	☐ RELAXED
☐ TIRED	☐ SLUGGISH	☐ WELL-RESTED
☐ REFRESHED	☐ FATIGUED	☐ JITTERY
☐ WEAK	☐ NUMB	☐ STRONG
☐ _____	☐ _____	☐ _____

Concentration / Focus:

NO ABILITY TO FOCUS   1   2   3   4   5   6   7   8   9   10   VERY FOCUSED

SOCIAL ENGAGEMENT	
Who did I see today?	How did I feel in their company?

☐ I preferred to be alone today

When we practice mindfulness, we bring our attention to the present moment. When we are truly in the present moment, it is difficult for our minds to be fixated on the past or anxious about the future. Grounding yourself in the present moment can help quiet your busy mind. By bringing your awareness to your senses, you can focus on the here and now. Start by identifying one thing you see in your space, notice what you feel supporting your body, and gently bring your attention to what you hear, taste, and smell. If you are unable to utilize certain senses, simply focus on those senses you are able to recognize. Does your mind feel calmer?

DAILY TRACKER

Today's Date: _____

Went to sleep at: _____ Woke up at: _____ Total hours slept: _____

MOOD / FEELINGS TRACKER			
	Start of Day	Middle of Day	End of Day
Notes			

TRIGGER TRACKER			
Time	Trigger	How did I respond?	What did I feel?

Physical Symptoms:

☐ ENERGIZED	☐ ACHY	☐ RELAXED
☐ TIRED	☐ SLUGGISH	☐ WELL-RESTED
☐ REFRESHED	☐ FATIGUED	☐ JITTERY
☐ WEAK	☐ NUMB	☐ STRONG
☐ _____	☐ _____	☐ _____

Concentration / Focus:

NO ABILITY TO FOCUS 1 2 3 4 5 6 7 8 9 10 VERY FOCUSED

SOCIAL ENGAGEMENT	
Who did I see today?	How did I feel in their company?

☐ I preferred to be alone today

What core values are most important to you? How can you put these into practice?

_____

_____

_____

_____

_____

_____

_____

_____

_____

_____

_____

_____

_____

_____

DAILY TRACKER

Today's Date: _____

Went to sleep at: _____ Woke up at: _____ Total hours slept: _____

MOOD / FEELINGS TRACKER			
	Start of Day	Middle of Day	End of Day
Notes			

TRIGGER TRACKER			
Time	Trigger	How did I respond?	What did I feel?

Physical Symptoms:

☐ ENERGIZED	☐ ACHY	☐ RELAXED
☐ TIRED	☐ SLUGGISH	☐ WELL-RESTED
☐ REFRESHED	☐ FATIGUED	☐ JITTERY
☐ WEAK	☐ NUMB	☐ STRONG
☐ _____	☐ _____	☐ _____

Concentration / Focus:

NO ABILITY TO FOCUS   1   2   3   4   5   6   7   8   9   10   VERY FOCUSED

SOCIAL ENGAGEMENT	
Who did I see today?	How did I feel in their company?

☐ I preferred to be alone today

What are you most proud of accomplishing in your life? How does this make you feel?

DAILY TRACKER

Today's Date: _____

Went to sleep at: _____ Woke up at: _____ Total hours slept: _____

MOOD / FEELINGS TRACKER			
	Start of Day	Middle of Day	End of Day
Notes			

TRIGGER TRACKER			
Time	Trigger	How did I respond?	What did I feel?

Physical Symptoms:

☐ ENERGIZED	☐ ACHY	☐ RELAXED
☐ TIRED	☐ SLUGGISH	☐ WELL-RESTED
☐ REFRESHED	☐ FATIGUED	☐ JITTERY
☐ WEAK	☐ NUMB	☐ STRONG
☐ _____	☐ _____	☐ _____

Concentration / Focus:

NO ABILITY TO FOCUS   1   2   3   4   5   6   7   8   9   10   VERY FOCUSED

SOCIAL ENGAGEMENT	
Who did I see today?	How did I feel in their company?

☐ I preferred to be alone today

What is the biggest challenge you have overcome? How did you do it?

DAILY TRACKER

Today's Date: _____

Went to sleep at: _____   Woke up at: _____   Total hours slept: _____

MOOD / FEELINGS TRACKER			
	Start of Day	Middle of Day	End of Day
Notes			

TRIGGER TRACKER			
Time	Trigger	How did I respond?	What did I feel?

Physical Symptoms:

☐ ENERGIZED	☐ ACHY	☐ RELAXED
☐ TIRED	☐ SLUGGISH	☐ WELL-RESTED
☐ REFRESHED	☐ FATIGUED	☐ JITTERY
☐ WEAK	☐ NUMB	☐ STRONG
☐ _____	☐ _____	☐ _____

Concentration / Focus:

NO ABILITY TO FOCUS   1   2   3   4   5   6   7   8   9   10   VERY FOCUSED

SOCIAL ENGAGEMENT	
Who did I see today?	How did I feel in their company?

☐ I preferred to be alone today

What makes you feel most loved and celebrated?

DAILY TRACKER

Today's Date: _____

Went to sleep at: _____   Woke up at: _____   Total hours slept: _____

MOOD / FEELINGS TRACKER			
	Start of Day	Middle of Day	End of Day
Notes			

TRIGGER TRACKER			
Time	Trigger	How did I respond?	What did I feel?

Physical Symptoms:

- ☐ ENERGIZED
- ☐ TIRED
- ☐ REFRESHED
- ☐ WEAK
- ☐ _____

- ☐ ACHY
- ☐ SLUGGISH
- ☐ FATIGUED
- ☐ NUMB
- ☐ _____

- ☐ RELAXED
- ☐ WELL-RESTED
- ☐ JITTERY
- ☐ STRONG
- ☐ _____

Concentration / Focus:

NO ABILITY TO FOCUS   1   2   3   4   5   6   7   8   9   10   VERY FOCUSED

SOCIAL ENGAGEMENT	
Who did I see today?	How did I feel in their company?

☐ I preferred to be alone today

HEALTHY HABIT

When we are feeling depressed, it can be easy to want to disconnect from others, but this is exactly when connection can help the most. Create a list of supportive friends and/or family you can lean on when you are struggling or having a hard day. Reach out to these people to ask them if it is okay to have them on your list and let them know how you like to receive support. Some of us like to just have someone listen, while others appreciate a more active approach. Our supporters are not mind readers, so let yours know what you prefer.

DAILY TRACKER

Today's Date: _____

Went to sleep at: _____ Woke up at: _____ Total hours slept: _____

MOOD / FEELINGS TRACKER			
	Start of Day	Middle of Day	End of Day
Notes			

TRIGGER TRACKER			
Time	Trigger	How did I respond?	What did I feel?

Physical Symptoms:

☐ ENERGIZED   ☐ ACHY   ☐ RELAXED
☐ TIRED   ☐ SLUGGISH   ☐ WELL-RESTED
☐ REFRESHED   ☐ FATIGUED   ☐ JITTERY
☐ WEAK   ☐ NUMB   ☐ STRONG
☐ _____   ☐ _____   ☐ _____

Concentration / Focus:

NO ABILITY TO FOCUS   1   2   3   4   5   6   7   8   9   10   VERY FOCUSED

SOCIAL ENGAGEMENT	
Who did I see today?	How did I feel in their company?

☐ I preferred to be alone today

Who do you count on most in your life? How do they show up for you?

DAILY TRACKER

Today's Date: _____

Went to sleep at: _____ Woke up at: _____ Total hours slept: _____

MOOD / FEELINGS TRACKER			
	Start of Day	Middle of Day	End of Day
Notes			

TRIGGER TRACKER			
Time	Trigger	How did I respond?	What did I feel?

Physical Symptoms:

☐ ENERGIZED   ☐ ACHY   ☐ RELAXED
☐ TIRED   ☐ SLUGGISH   ☐ WELL-RESTED
☐ REFRESHED   ☐ FATIGUED   ☐ JITTERY
☐ WEAK   ☐ NUMB   ☐ STRONG
☐ _____   ☐ _____   ☐ _____

Concentration / Focus:

NO ABILITY TO FOCUS | 1   2   3   4   5   6   7   8   9   10 | VERY FOCUSED

SOCIAL ENGAGEMENT	
Who did I see today?	How did I feel in their company?

☐ I preferred to be alone today

What are some things that you want to or need to let go of in your life?

DAILY TRACKER

Today's Date: _____

Went to sleep at: _____ Woke up at: _____ Total hours slept: _____

MOOD / FEELINGS TRACKER			
	Start of Day	Middle of Day	End of Day
Notes			

TRIGGER TRACKER			
Time	Trigger	How did I respond?	What did I feel?

Physical Symptoms:

☐ ENERGIZED	☐ ACHY	☐ RELAXED
☐ TIRED	☐ SLUGGISH	☐ WELL-RESTED
☐ REFRESHED	☐ FATIGUED	☐ JITTERY
☐ WEAK	☐ NUMB	☐ STRONG
☐ _____	☐ _____	☐ _____

Concentration / Focus:

NO ABILITY TO FOCUS 1 2 3 4 5 6 7 8 9 10 VERY FOCUSED

SOCIAL ENGAGEMENT	
Who did I see today?	How did I feel in their company?

☐ I preferred to be alone today

What is the most memorable lesson you have learned? Who taught it to you?

DAILY TRACKER

Today's Date: _____

Went to sleep at: _____ Woke up at: _____ Total hours slept: _____

MOOD / FEELINGS TRACKER			
	Start of Day	Middle of Day	End of Day
Notes			

TRIGGER TRACKER			
Time	Trigger	How did I respond?	What did I feel?

Physical Symptoms:

☐ ENERGIZED   ☐ ACHY   ☐ RELAXED

☐ TIRED   ☐ SLUGGISH   ☐ WELL-RESTED

☐ REFRESHED   ☐ FATIGUED   ☐ JITTERY

☐ WEAK   ☐ NUMB   ☐ STRONG

☐ _____   ☐ _____   ☐ _____

Concentration / Focus:

NO ABILITY TO FOCUS   1   2   3   4   5   6   7   8   9   10   VERY FOCUSED

SOCIAL ENGAGEMENT	
Who did I see today?	How did I feel in their company?

☐ I preferred to be alone today

How do you manage failure? Are there ways you can be gentler with yourself during these times?

DAILY TRACKER

Today's Date:

Went to sleep at: _____ Woke up at: _____ Total hours slept: _____

MOOD / FEELINGS TRACKER

	Start of Day	Middle of Day	End of Day
Notes			

TRIGGER TRACKER

Time	Trigger	How did I respond?	What did I feel?

Physical Symptoms:

☐ ENERGIZED   ☐ ACHY   ☐ RELAXED
☐ TIRED   ☐ SLUGGISH   ☐ WELL-RESTED
☐ REFRESHED   ☐ FATIGUED   ☐ JITTERY
☐ WEAK   ☐ NUMB   ☐ STRONG
☐   ☐   ☐

Concentration / Focus:

NO ABILITY TO FOCUS   1   2   3   4   5   6   7   8   9   10   VERY FOCUSED

SOCIAL ENGAGEMENT

Who did I see today?	How did I feel in their company?

☐ I preferred to be alone today

HEALTHY HABIT

Get your body moving. Exercise improves both our physical health and our mental health. You do not need to invest in a gym membership or workout equipment—you can start small. Begin by incorporating a five-minute stroll around the neighborhood, or consider a gentle online yoga class. Research shows that the area of the brain that regulates mood is smaller in those who are experiencing depression. Exercise has been shown to help with nerve growth and connection in this area of the brain, thus bringing some relief to depressive feelings.

DAILY TRACKER

Today's Date: _____

Went to sleep at: _____ Woke up at: _____ Total hours slept: _____

MOOD / FEELINGS TRACKER			
	Start of Day	Middle of Day	End of Day
Notes			

TRIGGER TRACKER			
Time	Trigger	How did I respond?	What did I feel?

Physical Symptoms:

☐ ENERGIZED	☐ ACHY	☐ RELAXED
☐ TIRED	☐ SLUGGISH	☐ WELL-RESTED
☐ REFRESHED	☐ FATIGUED	☐ JITTERY
☐ WEAK	☐ NUMB	☐ STRONG
☐ _____	☐ _____	☐ _____

Concentration / Focus:

NO ABILITY TO FOCUS 1 2 3 4 5 6 7 8 9 10 VERY FOCUSED

SOCIAL ENGAGEMENT	
Who did I see today?	How did I feel in their company?

☐ I preferred to be alone today

What is your greatest strength? How does it serve you?

DAILY TRACKER

Today's Date: _____

Went to sleep at: _____ Woke up at: _____ Total hours slept: _____

MOOD / FEELINGS TRACKER			
	Start of Day	Middle of Day	End of Day
Notes			

TRIGGER TRACKER			
Time	Trigger	How did I respond?	What did I feel?

Physical Symptoms:

☐ ENERGIZED	☐ ACHY	☐ RELAXED
☐ TIRED	☐ SLUGGISH	☐ WELL-RESTED
☐ REFRESHED	☐ FATIGUED	☐ JITTERY
☐ WEAK	☐ NUMB	☐ STRONG
☐ _____	☐ _____	☐ _____

Concentration / Focus:

NO ABILITY TO FOCUS   1   2   3   4   5   6   7   8   9   10   VERY FOCUSED

SOCIAL ENGAGEMENT	
Who did I see today?	How did I feel in their company?

☐ I preferred to be alone today

Who are you most inspired by? Why?

DAILY TRACKER

Today's Date: _____

Went to sleep at: _____   Woke up at: _____   Total hours slept: _____

MOOD / FEELINGS TRACKER

	Start of Day	Middle of Day	End of Day
Notes			

TRIGGER TRACKER

Time	Trigger	How did I respond?	What did I feel?

Physical Symptoms:

- ☐ ENERGIZED
- ☐ TIRED
- ☐ REFRESHED
- ☐ WEAK
- ☐ _____

- ☐ ACHY
- ☐ SLUGGISH
- ☐ FATIGUED
- ☐ NUMB
- ☐ _____

- ☐ RELAXED
- ☐ WELL-RESTED
- ☐ JITTERY
- ☐ STRONG
- ☐ _____

Concentration / Focus:

NO ABILITY TO FOCUS | 1 2 3 4 5 6 7 8 9 10 | VERY FOCUSED

SOCIAL ENGAGEMENT

Who did I see today?	How did I feel in their company?

☐ I preferred to be alone today

Who are the five people you spend the most time with? What energy do they bring into your life?

DAILY TRACKER

Today's Date: ....

Went to sleep at: .... Woke up at: .... Total hours slept: ....

MOOD / FEELINGS TRACKER			
	Start of Day	Middle of Day	End of Day
Notes			

TRIGGER TRACKER			
Time	Trigger	How did I respond?	What did I feel?

Physical Symptoms:

☐ ENERGIZED	☐ ACHY	☐ RELAXED
☐ TIRED	☐ SLUGGISH	☐ WELL-RESTED
☐ REFRESHED	☐ FATIGUED	☐ JITTERY
☐ WEAK	☐ NUMB	☐ STRONG
☐	☐	☐ ....

Concentration / Focus:

NO ABILITY TO FOCUS   1   2   3   4   5   6   7   8   9   10   VERY FOCUSED

SOCIAL ENGAGEMENT	
Who did I see today?	How did I feel in their company?

☐ I preferred to be alone today

What limiting beliefs do you hold about yourself that are stopping you from making changes in your life?

DAILY TRACKER

Today's Date: _____

Went to sleep at: _____ Woke up at: _____ Total hours slept: _____

MOOD / FEELINGS TRACKER			
	Start of Day	Middle of Day	End of Day
Notes			

TRIGGER TRACKER			
Time	Trigger	How did I respond?	What did I feel?

Physical Symptoms:

☐ ENERGIZED	☐ ACHY	☐ RELAXED
☐ TIRED	☐ SLUGGISH	☐ WELL-RESTED
☐ REFRESHED	☐ FATIGUED	☐ JITTERY
☐ WEAK	☐ NUMB	☐ STRONG
☐ _____	☐ _____	☐ _____

Concentration / Focus:

NO ABILITY TO FOCUS 1 2 3 4 5 6 7 8 9 10 VERY FOCUSED

SOCIAL ENGAGEMENT	
Who did I see today?	How did I feel in their company?

☐ I preferred to be alone today

HEALTHY HABIT

Meditation allows us to slow down, focus our attention, and quiet our busy minds. Begin by finding a comfortable position. You can sit upright, lie down, or adopt any other posture that works for your body. Gently close your eyes or lower your gaze. Start to notice your breath by placing a hand on your belly or chest and feeling the rise and fall of your body as you inhale and exhale. Try to simply focus on your breathing; if you notice your mind starting to wander, bring your attention back to your breath.

DAILY TRACKER

Today's Date: _____

Went to sleep at: _____ Woke up at: _____ Total hours slept: _____

MOOD / FEELINGS TRACKER			
	Start of Day	Middle of Day	End of Day
Notes			

TRIGGER TRACKER			
Time	Trigger	How did I respond?	What did I feel?

Physical Symptoms:

- ☐ ENERGIZED
- ☐ TIRED
- ☐ REFRESHED
- ☐ WEAK
- ☐ _____

- ☐ ACHY
- ☐ SLUGGISH
- ☐ FATIGUED
- ☐ NUMB
- ☐ _____

- ☐ RELAXED
- ☐ WELL-RESTED
- ☐ JITTERY
- ☐ STRONG
- ☐ _____

Concentration / Focus:

NO ABILITY TO FOCUS   1   2   3   4   5   6   7   8   9   10   VERY FOCUSED

SOCIAL ENGAGEMENT	
Who did I see today?	How did I feel in their company?

☐ I preferred to be alone today

Where do your limiting beliefs stem from? What are your earliest or most prominent memories of where these stories were created?

DAILY TRACKER

Today's Date: _____

Went to sleep at: _____ Woke up at: _____ Total hours slept: _____

MOOD / FEELINGS TRACKER			
	Start of Day	Middle of Day	End of Day
Notes			

TRIGGER TRACKER			
Time	Trigger	How did I respond?	What did I feel?

Physical Symptoms:

☐ ENERGIZED   ☐ ACHY   ☐ RELAXED
☐ TIRED   ☐ SLUGGISH   ☐ WELL-RESTED
☐ REFRESHED   ☐ FATIGUED   ☐ JITTERY
☐ WEAK   ☐ NUMB   ☐ STRONG
☐ _____   ☐ _____   ☐ _____

Concentration / Focus:

NO ABILITY TO FOCUS   1   2   3   4   5   6   7   8   9   10   VERY FOCUSED

SOCIAL ENGAGEMENT	
Who did I see today?	How did I feel in their company?

☐ I preferred to be alone today

What would your perfect day off look like?

DAILY TRACKER

Today's Date: _____

Went to sleep at: _____   Woke up at: _____   Total hours slept: _____

MOOD / FEELINGS TRACKER			
	Start of Day	Middle of Day	End of Day
Notes			

TRIGGER TRACKER			
Time	Trigger	How did I respond?	What did I feel?

Physical Symptoms:

☐ ENERGIZED   ☐ ACHY   ☐ RELAXED

☐ TIRED   ☐ SLUGGISH   ☐ WELL-RESTED

☐ REFRESHED   ☐ FATIGUED   ☐ JITTERY

☐ WEAK   ☐ NUMB   ☐ STRONG

☐ _____   ☐ _____   ☐ _____

Concentration / Focus:

NO ABILITY TO FOCUS 1   2   3   4   5   6   7   8   9   10 VERY FOCUSED

SOCIAL ENGAGEMENT	
Who did I see today?	How did I feel in their company?

☐ I preferred to be alone today

What makes you feel the most empowered? How can you do more of it?

DAILY TRACKER

Today's Date: _____

Went to sleep at: _____   Woke up at: _____   Total hours slept: _____

MOOD / FEELINGS TRACKER			
	Start of Day	Middle of Day	End of Day
Notes			

TRIGGER TRACKER			
Time	Trigger	How did I respond?	What did I feel?

Physical Symptoms:

☐ ENERGIZED	☐ ACHY	☐ RELAXED
☐ TIRED	☐ SLUGGISH	☐ WELL-RESTED
☐ REFRESHED	☐ FATIGUED	☐ JITTERY
☐ WEAK	☐ NUMB	☐ STRONG
☐ _____	☐ _____	☐ _____

Concentration / Focus:

NO ABILITY TO FOCUS 1   2   3   4   5   6   7   8   9   10 VERY FOCUSED

SOCIAL ENGAGEMENT	
Who did I see today?	How did I feel in their company?

☐ I preferred to be alone today

What role does fear play in your life?

DAILY TRACKER

Today's Date: ....

Went to sleep at: .... Woke up at: .... Total hours slept: ....

MOOD / FEELINGS TRACKER			
	Start of Day	Middle of Day	End of Day
Notes			

TRIGGER TRACKER			
Time	Trigger	How did I respond?	What did I feel?

Physical Symptoms:

☐ ENERGIZED	☐ ACHY	☐ RELAXED
☐ TIRED	☐ SLUGGISH	☐ WELL-RESTED
☐ REFRESHED	☐ FATIGUED	☐ JITTERY
☐ WEAK	☐ NUMB	☐ STRONG
☐	☐	☐ ....

Concentration / Focus:

NO ABILITY TO FOCUS | 1 2 3 4 5 6 7 8 9 10 | VERY FOCUSED

SOCIAL ENGAGEMENT	
Who did I see today?	How did I feel in their company?

☐ I preferred to be alone today

HEALTHY HABIT

When we acknowledge things we are proud of doing throughout our day, it gives us a sense of accomplishment. Try writing down three things you are proud of yourself for doing at the end of each day. These can be as simple as taking a shower or cooking a meal, or as big as getting a promotion at work.

DAILY TRACKER

Today's Date:

Went to sleep at: _____ Woke up at: _____ Total hours slept: _____

MOOD / FEELINGS TRACKER			
	Start of Day	Middle of Day	End of Day
Notes			

TRIGGER TRACKER			
Time	Trigger	How did I respond?	What did I feel?

Physical Symptoms:

☐ ENERGIZED   ☐ ACHY   ☐ RELAXED

☐ TIRED   ☐ SLUGGISH   ☐ WELL-RESTED

☐ REFRESHED   ☐ FATIGUED   ☐ JITTERY

☐ WEAK   ☐ NUMB   ☐ STRONG

☐ _____   ☐ _____   ☐ _____

Concentration / Focus:

NO ABILITY TO FOCUS   1   2   3   4   5   6   7   8   9   10   VERY FOCUSED

SOCIAL ENGAGEMENT	
Who did I see today?	How did I feel in their company?

☐ I preferred to be alone today

Do you trust yourself? Why or why not?

DAILY TRACKER

Today's Date: ....

Went to sleep at: .... Woke up at: .... Total hours slept: ....

MOOD / FEELINGS TRACKER			
	Start of Day	Middle of Day	End of Day
Notes			

TRIGGER TRACKER			
Time	Trigger	How did I respond?	What did I feel?

Physical Symptoms:

☐ ENERGIZED	☐ ACHY	☐ RELAXED
☐ TIRED	☐ SLUGGISH	☐ WELL-RESTED
☐ REFRESHED	☐ FATIGUED	☐ JITTERY
☐ WEAK	☐ NUMB	☐ STRONG
☐	☐	☐ ....

Concentration / Focus:

NO ABILITY TO FOCUS   1   2   3   4   5   6   7   8   9   10   VERY FOCUSED

SOCIAL ENGAGEMENT	
Who did I see today?	How did I feel in their company?

☐ I preferred to be alone today

Are you happy in your career? What do you dream of doing?

DAILY TRACKER

Today's Date: _____

Went to sleep at: _____   Woke up at: _____   Total hours slept: _____

MOOD / FEELINGS TRACKER			
	Start of Day	Middle of Day	End of Day
Notes			

TRIGGER TRACKER			
Time	Trigger	How did I respond?	What did I feel?

Physical Symptoms:

☐ ENERGIZED	☐ ACHY	☐ RELAXED
☐ TIRED	☐ SLUGGISH	☐ WELL-RESTED
☐ REFRESHED	☐ FATIGUED	☐ JITTERY
☐ WEAK	☐ NUMB	☐ STRONG
☐ _____	☐ _____	☐ _____

Concentration / Focus:

NO ABILITY TO FOCUS 1   2   3   4   5   6   7   8   9   10 VERY FOCUSED

SOCIAL ENGAGEMENT	
Who did I see today?	How did I feel in their company?

☐ I preferred to be alone today

What does your perfect weekend look like? How can you make it a reality?

DAILY TRACKER

Today's Date: _____

Went to sleep at: _____   Woke up at: _____   Total hours slept: _____

MOOD / FEELINGS TRACKER			
	Start of Day	Middle of Day	End of Day
Notes			

TRIGGER TRACKER			
Time	Trigger	How did I respond?	What did I feel?

Physical Symptoms:

☐ ENERGIZED	☐ ACHY	☐ RELAXED
☐ TIRED	☐ SLUGGISH	☐ WELL-RESTED
☐ REFRESHED	☐ FATIGUED	☐ JITTERY
☐ WEAK	☐ NUMB	☐ STRONG
☐ _____	☐ _____	☐ _____

Concentration / Focus:

NO ABILITY TO FOCUS   1   2   3   4   5   6   7   8   9   10   VERY FOCUSED

SOCIAL ENGAGEMENT	
Who did I see today?	How did I feel in their company?

☐ I preferred to be alone today

What is something you have done to help someone else recently? How did it make you feel?

DAILY TRACKER

Today's Date: _____

Went to sleep at: _____ Woke up at: _____ Total hours slept: _____

MOOD / FEELINGS TRACKER			
	Start of Day	Middle of Day	End of Day
Notes			

TRIGGER TRACKER			
Time	Trigger	How did I respond?	What did I feel?

Physical Symptoms:

☐ ENERGIZED   ☐ ACHY   ☐ RELAXED

☐ TIRED   ☐ SLUGGISH   ☐ WELL-RESTED

☐ REFRESHED   ☐ FATIGUED   ☐ JITTERY

☐ WEAK   ☐ NUMB   ☐ STRONG

☐ _____   ☐ _____   ☐ _____

Concentration / Focus:

NO ABILITY TO FOCUS   1   2   3   4   5   6   7   8   9   10   VERY FOCUSED

SOCIAL ENGAGEMENT	
Who did I see today?	How did I feel in their company?

☐ I preferred to be alone today

HEALTHY HABIT

Remember to breathe. Schedule breaks in your day to pause and focus on your breath. Set your alarm for a specific time each day and use it as a reminder to stop and breathe. Box breathing is a technique that can help calm the nervous system and decrease stress in your body. You can practice box breathing by inhaling for a count of four, holding your breath at the top for a count of four, slowly exhaling for a count of four, and then holding your breath at the bottom for a count of four. Repeat this for a total of four rounds and notice how you feel.

DAILY TRACKER

Today's Date: ....

Went to sleep at: .... Woke up at: .... Total hours slept: ....

MOOD / FEELINGS TRACKER			
	Start of Day	Middle of Day	End of Day
Notes			

TRIGGER TRACKER			
Time	Trigger	How did I respond?	What did I feel?

Physical Symptoms:

☐ ENERGIZED	☐ ACHY	☐ RELAXED
☐ TIRED	☐ SLUGGISH	☐ WELL-RESTED
☐ REFRESHED	☐ FATIGUED	☐ JITTERY
☐ WEAK	☐ NUMB	☐ STRONG
☐	☐	☐ ....

Concentration / Focus:

NO ABILITY TO FOCUS 1 2 3 4 5 6 7 8 9 10 VERY FOCUSED

SOCIAL ENGAGEMENT	
Who did I see today?	How did I feel in their company?

☐ I preferred to be alone today

What is one small commitment you can make to yourself today that will leave you feeling proud?

DAILY TRACKER

Today's Date: _____

Went to sleep at: _____ Woke up at: _____ Total hours slept: _____

MOOD / FEELINGS TRACKER			
	Start of Day	Middle of Day	End of Day
Notes			

TRIGGER TRACKER			
Time	Trigger	How did I respond?	What did I feel?

Physical Symptoms:

☐ ENERGIZED   ☐ ACHY   ☐ RELAXED

☐ TIRED   ☐ SLUGGISH   ☐ WELL-RESTED

☐ REFRESHED   ☐ FATIGUED   ☐ JITTERY

☐ WEAK   ☐ NUMB   ☐ STRONG

☐ _____   ☐ _____   ☐ _____

Concentration / Focus:

NO ABILITY TO FOCUS 1   2   3   4   5   6   7   8   9   10 VERY FOCUSED

SOCIAL ENGAGEMENT	
Who did I see today?	How did I feel in their company?

☐ I preferred to be alone today

Who or what makes you laugh the most? Why?

DAILY TRACKER

Today's Date: _____

Went to sleep at: _____ Woke up at: _____ Total hours slept: _____

MOOD / FEELINGS TRACKER			
	Start of Day	Middle of Day	End of Day
Notes			

TRIGGER TRACKER			
Time	Trigger	How did I respond?	What did I feel?

Physical Symptoms:

☐ ENERGIZED	☐ ACHY	☐ RELAXED
☐ TIRED	☐ SLUGGISH	☐ WELL-RESTED
☐ REFRESHED	☐ FATIGUED	☐ JITTERY
☐ WEAK	☐ NUMB	☐ STRONG
☐ _____	☐ _____	☐ _____

Concentration / Focus:

NO ABILITY TO FOCUS   1   2   3   4   5   6   7   8   9   10   VERY FOCUSED

SOCIAL ENGAGEMENT	
Who did I see today?	How did I feel in their company?

☐ I preferred to be alone today

What is a problem you have overcome? How did you do it?

DAILY TRACKER

Today's Date: _____

Went to sleep at: _____ Woke up at: _____ Total hours slept: _____

MOOD / FEELINGS TRACKER			
	Start of Day	Middle of Day	End of Day
Notes			

TRIGGER TRACKER			
Time	Trigger	How did I respond?	What did I feel?

Physical Symptoms:

□ ENERGIZED   □ ACHY   □ RELAXED
□ TIRED   □ SLUGGISH   □ WELL-RESTED
□ REFRESHED   □ FATIGUED   □ JITTERY
□ WEAK   □ NUMB   □ STRONG
□ _____   □ _____   □ _____

Concentration / Focus:

NO ABILITY TO FOCUS 1 2 3 4 5 6 7 8 9 10 VERY FOCUSED

SOCIAL ENGAGEMENT	
Who did I see today?	How did I feel in their company?

□ I preferred to be alone today

What do you wish your younger self knew? Write a letter to them here.

DAILY TRACKER

Today's Date: _____

Went to sleep at: _____ Woke up at: _____ Total hours slept: _____

MOOD / FEELINGS TRACKER			
	Start of Day	Middle of Day	End of Day
Notes			

TRIGGER TRACKER			
Time	Trigger	How did I respond?	What did I feel?

Physical Symptoms:

☐ ENERGIZED	☐ ACHY	☐ RELAXED
☐ TIRED	☐ SLUGGISH	☐ WELL-RESTED
☐ REFRESHED	☐ FATIGUED	☐ JITTERY
☐ WEAK	☐ NUMB	☐ STRONG
☐ _____	☐ _____	☐ _____

Concentration / Focus:

NO ABILITY TO FOCUS   1   2   3   4   5   6   7   8   9   10   VERY FOCUSED

SOCIAL ENGAGEMENT	
Who did I see today?	How did I feel in their company?

☐ I preferred to be alone today

HEALTHY HABIT

Create more opportunities for gratitude. Notice the words you use. For example, we often say that we "have to" eat dinner or that we "have to" take a shower. Our lives become lists of "have to's." Begin by replacing the words "have to" with "get to," and pay attention to how that shifts the statement into a place of gratitude. For example, "I 'get to' eat dinner" or "I 'get to' take a shower."

DAILY TRACKER

Today's Date: _____

Went to sleep at: _____ Woke up at: _____ Total hours slept: _____

MOOD / FEELINGS TRACKER			
	Start of Day	Middle of Day	End of Day
Notes			

TRIGGER TRACKER			
Time	Trigger	How did I respond?	What did I feel?

Physical Symptoms:

☐ ENERGIZED   ☐ ACHY   ☐ RELAXED

☐ TIRED   ☐ SLUGGISH   ☐ WELL-RESTED

☐ REFRESHED   ☐ FATIGUED   ☐ JITTERY

☐ WEAK   ☐ NUMB   ☐ STRONG

☐ _____   ☐ _____   ☐ _____

Concentration / Focus:

NO ABILITY TO FOCUS   1   2   3   4   5   6   7   8   9   10   VERY FOCUSED

SOCIAL ENGAGEMENT	
Who did I see today?	How did I feel in their company?

☐ I preferred to be alone today

Who is your biggest supporter? What does this person mean to you?

DAILY TRACKER

Today's Date: _____

Went to sleep at: _____ Woke up at: _____ Total hours slept: _____

MOOD / FEELINGS TRACKER			
	Start of Day	Middle of Day	End of Day
Notes			

TRIGGER TRACKER			
Time	Trigger	How did I respond?	What did I feel?

Physical Symptoms:

☐ ENERGIZED ☐ ACHY ☐ RELAXED

☐ TIRED ☐ SLUGGISH ☐ WELL-RESTED

☐ REFRESHED ☐ FATIGUED ☐ JITTERY

☐ WEAK ☐ NUMB ☐ STRONG

☐ _____ ☐ _____ ☐ _____

Concentration / Focus:

NO ABILITY TO FOCUS 1 2 3 4 5 6 7 8 9 10 VERY FOCUSED

SOCIAL ENGAGEMENT	
Who did I see today?	How did I feel in their company?

☐ I preferred to be alone today

What do you wish more people knew about you? Why is this important to you?

DAILY TRACKER

Today's Date: _____

Went to sleep at: _____ Woke up at: _____ Total hours slept: _____

MOOD / FEELINGS TRACKER			
	Start of Day	Middle of Day	End of Day
Notes			

TRIGGER TRACKER			
Time	Trigger	How did I respond?	What did I feel?

Physical Symptoms:

☐ ENERGIZED	☐ ACHY	☐ RELAXED
☐ TIRED	☐ SLUGGISH	☐ WELL-RESTED
☐ REFRESHED	☐ FATIGUED	☐ JITTERY
☐ WEAK	☐ NUMB	☐ STRONG
☐ _____	☐ _____	☐ _____

Concentration / Focus:

NO ABILITY TO FOCUS 1 2 3 4 5 6 7 8 9 10 VERY FOCUSED

SOCIAL ENGAGEMENT	
Who did I see today?	How did I feel in their company?

☐ I preferred to be alone today

When was the last time you cried? How did you feel afterward?

DAILY TRACKER

Today's Date: _____

Went to sleep at: _____ Woke up at: _____ Total hours slept: _____

MOOD / FEELINGS TRACKER			
	Start of Day	Middle of Day	End of Day
Notes			

TRIGGER TRACKER			
Time	Trigger	How did I respond?	What did I feel?

Physical Symptoms:

☐ ENERGIZED	☐ ACHY	☐ RELAXED
☐ TIRED	☐ SLUGGISH	☐ WELL-RESTED
☐ REFRESHED	☐ FATIGUED	☐ JITTERY
☐ WEAK	☐ NUMB	☐ STRONG
☐ _____	☐ _____	☐ _____

Concentration / Focus:

NO ABILITY TO FOCUS   1   2   3   4   5   6   7   8   9   10   VERY FOCUSED

SOCIAL ENGAGEMENT	
Who did I see today?	How did I feel in their company?

☐ I preferred to be alone today

92   DEPRESSION JOURNAL: DAILY CHECK-IN

Write yourself a love letter, then describe how it made you feel
to write it.

DAILY TRACKER

Today's Date: _____

Went to sleep at: _____ Woke up at: _____ Total hours slept: _____

MOOD / FEELINGS TRACKER			
	Start of Day	Middle of Day	End of Day
Notes			

TRIGGER TRACKER			
Time	Trigger	How did I respond?	What did I feel?

Physical Symptoms:

☐ ENERGIZED   ☐ ACHY   ☐ RELAXED
☐ TIRED   ☐ SLUGGISH   ☐ WELL-RESTED
☐ REFRESHED   ☐ FATIGUED   ☐ JITTERY
☐ WEAK   ☐ NUMB   ☐ STRONG
☐ _____   ☐ _____   ☐ _____

Concentration / Focus:

NO ABILITY TO FOCUS 1   2   3   4   5   6   7   8   9   10 VERY FOCUSED

SOCIAL ENGAGEMENT	
Who did I see today?	How did I feel in their company?

☐ I preferred to be alone today

HEALTHY HABIT

Continue to learn. Research shows that taking in new information increases our mental well-being. Set a timer for 10 minutes and listen to a podcast, read a book, pick up a newspaper, or simply research a topic you are interested in online. Notice what you have learned in a short amount of time. How does it feel to have learned something new?

DAILY TRACKER

Today's Date: ....

Went to sleep at: .... Woke up at: .... Total hours slept: ....

MOOD / FEELINGS TRACKER			
	Start of Day	Middle of Day	End of Day
Notes			

TRIGGER TRACKER			
Time	Trigger	How did I respond?	What did I feel?

Physical Symptoms:

☐ ENERGIZED   ☐ ACHY   ☐ RELAXED

☐ TIRED   ☐ SLUGGISH   ☐ WELL-RESTED

☐ REFRESHED   ☐ FATIGUED   ☐ JITTERY

☐ WEAK   ☐ NUMB   ☐ STRONG

☐ ....   ☐ ....   ☐ ....

Concentration / Focus:

NO ABILITY TO FOCUS 1   2   3   4   5   6   7   8   9   10 VERY FOCUSED

SOCIAL ENGAGEMENT	
Who did I see today?	How did I feel in their company?

☐ I preferred to be alone today

What is the kindest thing someone has done for you?

DAILY TRACKER

Today's Date: ....

Went to sleep at: .... Woke up at: .... Total hours slept: ....

MOOD / FEELINGS TRACKER			
	Start of Day	Middle of Day	End of Day
Notes			

TRIGGER TRACKER			
Time	Trigger	How did I respond?	What did I feel?

Physical Symptoms:

☐ ENERGIZED   ☐ ACHY   ☐ RELAXED
☐ TIRED   ☐ SLUGGISH   ☐ WELL-RESTED
☐ REFRESHED   ☐ FATIGUED   ☐ JITTERY
☐ WEAK   ☐ NUMB   ☐ STRONG
☐ ....   ☐ ....   ☐ ....

Concentration / Focus:

NO ABILITY TO FOCUS   1   2   3   4   5   6   7   8   9   10   VERY FOCUSED

SOCIAL ENGAGEMENT	
Who did I see today?	How did I feel in their company?

☐ I preferred to be alone today

What is your favorite childhood memory? Why?

DAILY TRACKER

Today's Date: _____

Went to sleep at: _____ Woke up at: _____ Total hours slept: _____

MOOD / FEELINGS TRACKER			
	Start of Day	Middle of Day	End of Day
Notes			

TRIGGER TRACKER			
Time	Trigger	How did I respond?	What did I feel?

Physical Symptoms:

☐ ENERGIZED   ☐ ACHY   ☐ RELAXED
☐ TIRED   ☐ SLUGGISH   ☐ WELL-RESTED
☐ REFRESHED   ☐ FATIGUED   ☐ JITTERY
☐ WEAK   ☐ NUMB   ☐ STRONG
☐ _____   ☐ _____   ☐ _____

Concentration / Focus:

NO ABILITY TO FOCUS   1   2   3   4   5   6   7   8   9   10   VERY FOCUSED

SOCIAL ENGAGEMENT	
Who did I see today?	How did I feel in their company?

☐ I preferred to be alone today

How do you imagine your life would be if you did not experience depression?

DAILY TRACKER

Today's Date: ....

Went to sleep at: .... Woke up at: .... Total hours slept: ....

MOOD / FEELINGS TRACKER			
	Start of Day	Middle of Day	End of Day
Notes			

TRIGGER TRACKER			
Time	Trigger	How did I respond?	What did I feel?

Physical Symptoms:

☐ ENERGIZED   ☐ ACHY   ☐ RELAXED
☐ TIRED   ☐ SLUGGISH   ☐ WELL-RESTED
☐ REFRESHED   ☐ FATIGUED   ☐ JITTERY
☐ WEAK   ☐ NUMB   ☐ STRONG
☐   ☐   ☐

Concentration / Focus:

NO ABILITY   1   2   3   4   5   6   7   8   9   10   VERY
TO FOCUS   FOCUSED

SOCIAL ENGAGEMENT	
Who did I see today?	How did I feel in their company?

☐ I preferred to be alone today

What makes you feel the most anxious? What is one small thing you can do to combat it?

DAILY TRACKER

Today's Date: _____

Went to sleep at: _____ Woke up at: _____ Total hours slept: _____

MOOD / FEELINGS TRACKER			
	Start of Day	Middle of Day	End of Day
Notes			

TRIGGER TRACKER			
Time	Trigger	How did I respond?	What did I feel?

Physical Symptoms:

☐ ENERGIZED	☐ ACHY	☐ RELAXED
☐ TIRED	☐ SLUGGISH	☐ WELL-RESTED
☐ REFRESHED	☐ FATIGUED	☐ JITTERY
☐ WEAK	☐ NUMB	☐ STRONG
☐ _____	☐ _____	☐ _____

Concentration / Focus:

NO ABILITY TO FOCUS   1   2   3   4   5   6   7   8   9   10   VERY FOCUSED

SOCIAL ENGAGEMENT	
Who did I see today?	How did I feel in their company?

☐ I preferred to be alone today

HEALTHY HABIT

Get outside and experience nature. Go for a walk, find a hiking trail, rest by the water, or simply feel the grass between your bare toes. Take in the natural beauty that surrounds you. Notice the season, the color of the leaves, the temperature of the air, and how it feels to just be, without a need to change anything. Nature can be healing and help lower your stress, anxiety, and depression.

DAILY TRACKER

Today's Date: ....

Went to sleep at: .... Woke up at: .... Total hours slept: ....

MOOD / FEELINGS TRACKER			
	Start of Day	Middle of Day	End of Day
Notes			

TRIGGER TRACKER			
Time	Trigger	How did I respond?	What did I feel?

Physical Symptoms:

☐ ENERGIZED	☐ ACHY	☐ RELAXED
☐ TIRED	☐ SLUGGISH	☐ WELL-RESTED
☐ REFRESHED	☐ FATIGUED	☐ JITTERY
☐ WEAK	☐ NUMB	☐ STRONG
☐	☐	☐ ....

Concentration / Focus:

NO ABILITY TO FOCUS 1   2   3   4   5   6   7   8   9   10 VERY FOCUSED

SOCIAL ENGAGEMENT	
Who did I see today?	How did I feel in their company?

☐ I preferred to be alone today

What is the hardest thing you have had to do in your life? How did you get through it?

DAILY TRACKER

Today's Date: _____

Went to sleep at: _____   Woke up at: _____   Total hours slept: _____

MOOD / FEELINGS TRACKER			
	Start of Day	Middle of Day	End of Day
Notes			

TRIGGER TRACKER			
Time	Trigger	How did I respond?	What did I feel?

Physical Symptoms:

☐ ENERGIZED	☐ ACHY	☐ RELAXED
☐ TIRED	☐ SLUGGISH	☐ WELL-RESTED
☐ REFRESHED	☐ FATIGUED	☐ JITTERY
☐ WEAK	☐ NUMB	☐ STRONG
☐ _____	☐ _____	☐ _____

Concentration / Focus:

NO ABILITY TO FOCUS   1   2   3   4   5   6   7   8   9   10   VERY FOCUSED

SOCIAL ENGAGEMENT	
Who did I see today?	How did I feel in their company?

☐ I preferred to be alone today

What are three things that bring you joy? How can you do more of them?

DAILY TRACKER

Today's Date: _____

Went to sleep at: _____   Woke up at: _____   Total hours slept: _____

MOOD / FEELINGS TRACKER			
	Start of Day	Middle of Day	End of Day
Notes			

TRIGGER TRACKER			
Time	Trigger	How did I respond?	What did I feel?

Physical Symptoms:

☐ ENERGIZED	☐ ACHY	☐ RELAXED
☐ TIRED	☐ SLUGGISH	☐ WELL-RESTED
☐ REFRESHED	☐ FATIGUED	☐ JITTERY
☐ WEAK	☐ NUMB	☐ STRONG
☐ _____	☐ _____	☐ _____

Concentration / Focus:

NO ABILITY TO FOCUS   1   2   3   4   5   6   7   8   9   10   VERY FOCUSED

SOCIAL ENGAGEMENT	
Who did I see today?	How did I feel in their company?

☐ I preferred to be alone today

Who do you struggle to set healthy boundaries with? Why?

DAILY TRACKER

Today's Date: _____

Went to sleep at: _____ Woke up at: _____ Total hours slept: _____

MOOD / FEELINGS TRACKER			
	Start of Day	Middle of Day	End of Day
Notes			

TRIGGER TRACKER			
Time	Trigger	How did I respond?	What did I feel?

Physical Symptoms:

- ☐ ENERGIZED
- ☐ TIRED
- ☐ REFRESHED
- ☐ WEAK
- ☐ _____

- ☐ ACHY
- ☐ SLUGGISH
- ☐ FATIGUED
- ☐ NUMB
- ☐ _____

- ☐ RELAXED
- ☐ WELL-RESTED
- ☐ JITTERY
- ☐ STRONG
- ☐ _____

Concentration / Focus:

NO ABILITY TO FOCUS 1 2 3 4 5 6 7 8 9 10 VERY FOCUSED

SOCIAL ENGAGEMENT	
Who did I see today?	How did I feel in their company?

☐ I preferred to be alone today

What is one self-care ritual (other than journaling) you can implement into your daily routine?

DAILY TRACKER

Today's Date: _____

Went to sleep at: _____ Woke up at: _____ Total hours slept: _____

MOOD / FEELINGS TRACKER			
	Start of Day	Middle of Day	End of Day
Notes			

TRIGGER TRACKER			
Time	Trigger	How did I respond?	What did I feel?

Physical Symptoms:

- ☐ ENERGIZED
- ☐ TIRED
- ☐ REFRESHED
- ☐ WEAK
- ☐ _____

- ☐ ACHY
- ☐ SLUGGISH
- ☐ FATIGUED
- ☐ NUMB
- ☐ _____

- ☐ RELAXED
- ☐ WELL-RESTED
- ☐ JITTERY
- ☐ STRONG
- ☐ _____

Concentration / Focus:

NO ABILITY TO FOCUS   1   2   3   4   5   6   7   8   9   10   VERY FOCUSED

SOCIAL ENGAGEMENT	
Who did I see today?	How did I feel in their company?

☐ I preferred to be alone today

HEALTHY HABIT

Listen to some music and get lost in the rhythm and beat. Whether it is classical, rock, or rap, turn on a song that always makes you smile and reminds you of a happy time. Don't be afraid to turn up the volume and move your body if you feel so inclined. Extra points if you incorporate listening to your favorite song into your daily routine!

DAILY TRACKER

Today's Date: _____

Went to sleep at: _____ Woke up at: _____ Total hours slept: _____

MOOD / FEELINGS TRACKER			
	Start of Day	Middle of Day	End of Day
Notes			

TRIGGER TRACKER			
Time	Trigger	How did I respond?	What did I feel?

Physical Symptoms:

☐ ENERGIZED   ☐ ACHY   ☐ RELAXED

☐ TIRED   ☐ SLUGGISH   ☐ WELL-RESTED

☐ REFRESHED   ☐ FATIGUED   ☐ JITTERY

☐ WEAK   ☐ NUMB   ☐ STRONG

☐ _____   ☐ _____   ☐ _____

Concentration / Focus:

NO ABILITY TO FOCUS   1   2   3   4   5   6   7   8   9   10   VERY FOCUSED

SOCIAL ENGAGEMENT	
Who did I see today?	How did I feel in their company?

☐ I preferred to be alone today

What brings you the most comfort? Why?

DAILY TRACKER

Today's Date: _____

Went to sleep at: _____ Woke up at: _____ Total hours slept: _____

MOOD / FEELINGS TRACKER			
	Start of Day	Middle of Day	End of Day
Notes			

TRIGGER TRACKER			
Time	Trigger	How did I respond?	What did I feel?

Physical Symptoms:

☐ ENERGIZED	☐ ACHY	☐ RELAXED
☐ TIRED	☐ SLUGGISH	☐ WELL-RESTED
☐ REFRESHED	☐ FATIGUED	☐ JITTERY
☐ WEAK	☐ NUMB	☐ STRONG
☐ _____	☐ _____	☐ _____

Concentration / Focus:

NO ABILITY TO FOCUS   1   2   3   4   5   6   7   8   9   10   VERY FOCUSED

SOCIAL ENGAGEMENT	
Who did I see today?	How did I feel in their company?

☐ I preferred to be alone today

List any negative self-talk you experience, then write a counter statement for each item.

DAILY TRACKER

Today's Date: _____

Went to sleep at: _____ Woke up at: _____ Total hours slept: _____

MOOD / FEELINGS TRACKER			
	Start of Day	Middle of Day	End of Day
Notes			

TRIGGER TRACKER			
Time	Trigger	How did I respond?	What did I feel?

Physical Symptoms:

☐ ENERGIZED	☐ ACHY	☐ RELAXED
☐ TIRED	☐ SLUGGISH	☐ WELL-RESTED
☐ REFRESHED	☐ FATIGUED	☐ JITTERY
☐ WEAK	☐ NUMB	☐ STRONG
☐ _____	☐ _____	☐ _____

Concentration / Focus:

NO ABILITY TO FOCUS   1   2   3   4   5   6   7   8   9   10   VERY FOCUSED

SOCIAL ENGAGEMENT	
Who did I see today?	How did I feel in their company?

☐ I preferred to be alone today

When are you most self-critical? Why?

DAILY TRACKER

Today's Date: _____

Went to sleep at: _____ Woke up at: _____ Total hours slept: _____

MOOD / FEELINGS TRACKER			
	Start of Day	Middle of Day	End of Day
Notes			

TRIGGER TRACKER			
Time	Trigger	How did I respond?	What did I feel?

Physical Symptoms:

☐ ENERGIZED	☐ ACHY	☐ RELAXED
☐ TIRED	☐ SLUGGISH	☐ WELL-RESTED
☐ REFRESHED	☐ FATIGUED	☐ JITTERY
☐ WEAK	☐ NUMB	☐ STRONG
☐ _____	☐ _____	☐ _____

Concentration / Focus:

NO ABILITY TO FOCUS   1   2   3   4   5   6   7   8   9   10   VERY FOCUSED

SOCIAL ENGAGEMENT	
Who did I see today?	How did I feel in their company?

☐ I preferred to be alone today

What makes you feel the most confident? Why?

DAILY TRACKER

Today's Date: _____

Went to sleep at: _____ Woke up at: _____ Total hours slept: _____

MOOD / FEELINGS TRACKER			
	Start of Day	Middle of Day	End of Day
Notes			

TRIGGER TRACKER			
Time	Trigger	How did I respond?	What did I feel?

Physical Symptoms:

☐ ENERGIZED ☐ ACHY ☐ RELAXED
☐ TIRED ☐ SLUGGISH ☐ WELL-RESTED
☐ REFRESHED ☐ FATIGUED ☐ JITTERY
☐ WEAK ☐ NUMB ☐ STRONG
☐ _____ ☐ _____ ☐ _____

Concentration / Focus:

NO ABILITY TO FOCUS 1 2 3 4 5 6 7 8 9 10 VERY FOCUSED

SOCIAL ENGAGEMENT	
Who did I see today?	How did I feel in their company?

☐ I preferred to be alone today

HEALTHY HABIT

Maintain a healthy diet. What we put into our bodies matters and affects our overall well-being. Pay attention to what your body is telling you. Are you eating to satiate hunger, because you are feeling happy or sad, or to connect with your senses? As we become attuned to what our bodies need, we can begin to make incremental changes to better nourish ourselves.

DAILY TRACKER

Today's Date: _____

Went to sleep at: _____ Woke up at: _____ Total hours slept: _____

MOOD / FEELINGS TRACKER			
	Start of Day	Middle of Day	End of Day
Notes			

TRIGGER TRACKER			
Time	Trigger	How did I respond?	What did I feel?

Physical Symptoms:

☐ ENERGIZED   ☐ ACHY   ☐ RELAXED

☐ TIRED   ☐ SLUGGISH   ☐ WELL-RESTED

☐ REFRESHED   ☐ FATIGUED   ☐ JITTERY

☐ WEAK   ☐ NUMB   ☐ STRONG

☐ _____   ☐ _____   ☐ _____

Concentration / Focus:

NO ABILITY TO FOCUS 1   2   3   4   5   6   7   8   9   10 VERY FOCUSED

SOCIAL ENGAGEMENT	
Who did I see today?	How did I feel in their company?

☐ I preferred to be alone today

How do you find acceptance during difficult times? How can you use that self-comfort to support you right now?

DAILY TRACKER

Today's Date: _____

Went to sleep at: _____ Woke up at: _____ Total hours slept: _____

MOOD / FEELINGS TRACKER			
	Start of Day	Middle of Day	End of Day
Notes			

TRIGGER TRACKER			
Time	Trigger	How did I respond?	What did I feel?

Physical Symptoms:

☐ ENERGIZED   ☐ ACHY   ☐ RELAXED
☐ TIRED   ☐ SLUGGISH   ☐ WELL-RESTED
☐ REFRESHED   ☐ FATIGUED   ☐ JITTERY
☐ WEAK   ☐ NUMB   ☐ STRONG
☐ _____   ☐ _____   ☐ _____

Concentration / Focus:

NO ABILITY TO FOCUS   1   2   3   4   5   6   7   8   9   10   VERY FOCUSED

SOCIAL ENGAGEMENT	
Who did I see today?	How did I feel in their company?

☐ I preferred to be alone today

What is it like for you to sit with your emotions? What do you notice when you don't distract yourself from them?

DAILY TRACKER

Today's Date: _____

Went to sleep at: _____ Woke up at: _____ Total hours slept: _____

MOOD / FEELINGS TRACKER			
	Start of Day	Middle of Day	End of Day
Notes			

TRIGGER TRACKER			
Time	Trigger	How did I respond?	What did I feel?

Physical Symptoms:

☐ ENERGIZED	☐ ACHY	☐ RELAXED
☐ TIRED	☐ SLUGGISH	☐ WELL-RESTED
☐ REFRESHED	☐ FATIGUED	☐ JITTERY
☐ WEAK	☐ NUMB	☐ STRONG
☐ _____	☐ _____	☐ _____

Concentration / Focus:

NO ABILITY TO FOCUS   1   2   3   4   5   6   7   8   9   10   VERY FOCUSED

SOCIAL ENGAGEMENT	
Who did I see today?	How did I feel in their company?

☐ I preferred to be alone today

What is something you once beat yourself up about but can now laugh at?

DAILY TRACKER

Today's Date: _____

Went to sleep at: _____ Woke up at: _____ Total hours slept: _____

MOOD / FEELINGS TRACKER			
	Start of Day	Middle of Day	End of Day
Notes			

TRIGGER TRACKER			
Time	Trigger	How did I respond?	What did I feel?

Physical Symptoms:

☐ ENERGIZED	☐ ACHY	☐ RELAXED
☐ TIRED	☐ SLUGGISH	☐ WELL-RESTED
☐ REFRESHED	☐ FATIGUED	☐ JITTERY
☐ WEAK	☐ NUMB	☐ STRONG
☐ _____	☐ _____	☐ _____

Concentration / Focus:

NO ABILITY TO FOCUS   1   2   3   4   5   6   7   8   9   10   VERY FOCUSED

SOCIAL ENGAGEMENT	
Who did I see today?	How did I feel in their company?

☐ I preferred to be alone today

Who in your life would you describe as resilient? What can you learn from them?

_____

_____

_____

_____

_____

_____

_____

_____

_____

_____

_____

_____

_____

_____

DAILY TRACKER

Today's Date: ....

Went to sleep at: .... Woke up at: .... Total hours slept: ....

MOOD / FEELINGS TRACKER			
	Start of Day	Middle of Day	End of Day
Notes			

TRIGGER TRACKER			
Time	Trigger	How did I respond?	What did I feel?

Physical Symptoms:

☐ ENERGIZED	☐ ACHY	☐ RELAXED
☐ TIRED	☐ SLUGGISH	☐ WELL-RESTED
☐ REFRESHED	☐ FATIGUED	☐ JITTERY
☐ WEAK	☐ NUMB	☐ STRONG
☐	☐	☐ ....

Concentration / Focus:

NO ABILITY TO FOCUS 1 2 3 4 5 6 7 8 9 10 VERY FOCUSED

SOCIAL ENGAGEMENT	
Who did I see today?	How did I feel in their company?

☐ I preferred to be alone today

HEALTHY HABIT

Focusing outward and performing small acts of kindness can create feelings of purpose and help boost our moods. How can you be of service to someone? Perhaps you can take care of a neighbor's pet, carry someone's groceries to their car, help an elderly person cross the street, or simply ask a cashier how their day is going. It doesn't really matter what the act is, so long as you are helping someone else.

DAILY TRACKER

Today's Date: _____

Went to sleep at: _____ Woke up at: _____ Total hours slept: _____

MOOD / FEELINGS TRACKER			
	Start of Day	Middle of Day	End of Day
Notes			

TRIGGER TRACKER			
Time	Trigger	How did I respond?	What did I feel?

Physical Symptoms:

☐ ENERGIZED   ☐ ACHY   ☐ RELAXED

☐ TIRED   ☐ SLUGGISH   ☐ WELL-RESTED

☐ REFRESHED   ☐ FATIGUED   ☐ JITTERY

☐ WEAK   ☐ NUMB   ☐ STRONG

☐ _____   ☐ _____   ☐ _____

Concentration / Focus:

NO ABILITY TO FOCUS 1   2   3   4   5   6   7   8   9   10 VERY FOCUSED

SOCIAL ENGAGEMENT	
Who did I see today?	How did I feel in their company?

☐ I preferred to be alone today

Slow down and take five deep breaths. What do you notice happens in your body when you do this? How do you feel?

DAILY TRACKER

Today's Date: _____

Went to sleep at: _____ Woke up at: _____ Total hours slept: _____

MOOD / FEELINGS TRACKER

	Start of Day	Middle of Day	End of Day
Notes			

TRIGGER TRACKER

Time	Trigger	How did I respond?	What did I feel?

Physical Symptoms:

- ☐ ENERGIZED
- ☐ TIRED
- ☐ REFRESHED
- ☐ WEAK
- ☐ _____

- ☐ ACHY
- ☐ SLUGGISH
- ☐ FATIGUED
- ☐ NUMB
- ☐

- ☐ RELAXED
- ☐ WELL-RESTED
- ☐ JITTERY
- ☐ STRONG
- ☐ _____

Concentration / Focus:

NO ABILITY TO FOCUS 1 2 3 4 5 6 7 8 9 10 VERY FOCUSED

SOCIAL ENGAGEMENT

Who did I see today?	How did I feel in their company?

☐ I preferred to be alone today

If you were granted three wishes, what would you ask for? Why?

DAILY TRACKER

Today's Date: _____

Went to sleep at: _____ Woke up at: _____ Total hours slept: _____

MOOD / FEELINGS TRACKER			
	Start of Day	Middle of Day	End of Day
Notes			

TRIGGER TRACKER			
Time	Trigger	How did I respond?	What did I feel?

Physical Symptoms:

☐ ENERGIZED   ☐ ACHY   ☐ RELAXED

☐ TIRED   ☐ SLUGGISH   ☐ WELL-RESTED

☐ REFRESHED   ☐ FATIGUED   ☐ JITTERY

☐ WEAK   ☐ NUMB   ☐ STRONG

☐ _____   ☐ _____   ☐ _____

Concentration / Focus:

NO ABILITY TO FOCUS   1   2   3   4   5   6   7   8   9   10   VERY FOCUSED

SOCIAL ENGAGEMENT	
Who did I see today?	How did I feel in their company?

☐ I preferred to be alone today

What and/or who makes you feel the most appreciated? Why?

DAILY TRACKER

Today's Date: _____

Went to sleep at: _____ Woke up at: _____ Total hours slept: _____

MOOD / FEELINGS TRACKER			
	Start of Day	Middle of Day	End of Day
Notes			

TRIGGER TRACKER			
Time	Trigger	How did I respond?	What did I feel?

Physical Symptoms:

- ☐ ENERGIZED
- ☐ TIRED
- ☐ REFRESHED
- ☐ WEAK
- ☐ _____

- ☐ ACHY
- ☐ SLUGGISH
- ☐ FATIGUED
- ☐ NUMB
- ☐ _____

- ☐ RELAXED
- ☐ WELL-RESTED
- ☐ JITTERY
- ☐ STRONG
- ☐ _____

Concentration / Focus:

NO ABILITY TO FOCUS 1 2 3 4 5 6 7 8 9 10 VERY FOCUSED

SOCIAL ENGAGEMENT	
Who did I see today?	How did I feel in their company?

☐ I preferred to be alone today

What is one thing in your life that you enjoy? What can you do to develop more of it in your life?

_____

_____

_____

_____

_____

_____

_____

_____

_____

_____

_____

_____

_____

_____

DAILY TRACKER

Today's Date: _____

Went to sleep at: _____   Woke up at: _____   Total hours slept: _____

MOOD / FEELINGS TRACKER

	Start of Day	Middle of Day	End of Day
Notes			

TRIGGER TRACKER

Time	Trigger	How did I respond?	What did I feel?

Physical Symptoms:

☐ ENERGIZED	☐ ACHY	☐ RELAXED
☐ TIRED	☐ SLUGGISH	☐ WELL-RESTED
☐ REFRESHED	☐ FATIGUED	☐ JITTERY
☐ WEAK	☐ NUMB	☐ STRONG
☐ _____	☐ _____	☐ _____

Concentration / Focus:

NO ABILITY TO FOCUS   1   2   3   4   5   6   7   8   9   10   VERY FOCUSED

SOCIAL ENGAGEMENT

Who did I see today?	How did I feel in their company?

☐ I preferred to be alone today

HEALTHY HABIT

What makes you laugh? As they say, laughter is the best medicine. When we laugh, our bodies release endorphins, which act as natural painkillers and mood boosters. So go ahead and watch a funny movie, pull up some silly videos on your computer, or listen to your favorite comedian—and then notice what happens. Can you challenge yourself to laugh once a day?

DAILY TRACKER

Today's Date: _____

Went to sleep at: _____   Woke up at: _____   Total hours slept: _____

MOOD / FEELINGS TRACKER			
	Start of Day	Middle of Day	End of Day
Notes			

TRIGGER TRACKER			
Time	Trigger	How did I respond?	What did I feel?

Physical Symptoms:

☐ ENERGIZED	☐ ACHY	☐ RELAXED
☐ TIRED	☐ SLUGGISH	☐ WELL-RESTED
☐ REFRESHED	☐ FATIGUED	☐ JITTERY
☐ WEAK	☐ NUMB	☐ STRONG
☐ _____	☐ _____	☐ _____

Concentration / Focus:

NO ABILITY TO FOCUS   1   2   3   4   5   6   7   8   9   10   VERY FOCUSED

SOCIAL ENGAGEMENT	
Who did I see today?	How did I feel in their company?

☐ I preferred to be alone today

What is one thing you are looking forward to? Why?

DAILY TRACKER

Today's Date: _____

Went to sleep at: _____ Woke up at: _____ Total hours slept: _____

MOOD / FEELINGS TRACKER			
	Start of Day	Middle of Day	End of Day
Notes			

TRIGGER TRACKER			
Time	Trigger	How did I respond?	What did I feel?

Physical Symptoms:

☐ ENERGIZED   ☐ ACHY   ☐ RELAXED
☐ TIRED   ☐ SLUGGISH   ☐ WELL-RESTED
☐ REFRESHED   ☐ FATIGUED   ☐ JITTERY
☐ WEAK   ☐ NUMB   ☐ STRONG
☐ _____   ☐ _____   ☐ _____

Concentration / Focus:

NO ABILITY TO FOCUS |—1—2—3—4—5—6—7—8—9—10—| VERY FOCUSED

SOCIAL ENGAGEMENT	
Who did I see today?	How did I feel in their company?

☐ I preferred to be alone today

When is the last time you did something kind for yourself? How did it feel?

DAILY TRACKER

Today's Date: _____

Went to sleep at: _____ Woke up at: _____ Total hours slept: _____

MOOD / FEELINGS TRACKER			
	Start of Day	Middle of Day	End of Day
Notes			

TRIGGER TRACKER			
Time	Trigger	How did I respond?	What did I feel?

Physical Symptoms:

☐ ENERGIZED	☐ ACHY	☐ RELAXED
☐ TIRED	☐ SLUGGISH	☐ WELL-RESTED
☐ REFRESHED	☐ FATIGUED	☐ JITTERY
☐ WEAK	☐ NUMB	☐ STRONG
☐ _____	☐ _____	☐ _____

Concentration / Focus:

NO ABILITY TO FOCUS   1   2   3   4   5   6   7   8   9   10   VERY FOCUSED

SOCIAL ENGAGEMENT	
Who did I see today?	How did I feel in their company?

☐ I preferred to be alone today

What is one thing that went better than you expected in the last month?

_____

_____

_____

_____

_____

_____

_____

_____

_____

_____

_____

_____

_____

_____

DAILY TRACKER

Today's Date: _____

Went to sleep at: _____   Woke up at: _____   Total hours slept: _____

MOOD / FEELINGS TRACKER			
	Start of Day	Middle of Day	End of Day
Notes			

TRIGGER TRACKER			
Time	Trigger	How did I respond?	What did I feel?

Physical Symptoms:

☐ ENERGIZED   ☐ ACHY   ☐ RELAXED
☐ TIRED   ☐ SLUGGISH   ☐ WELL-RESTED
☐ REFRESHED   ☐ FATIGUED   ☐ JITTERY
☐ WEAK   ☐ NUMB   ☐ STRONG
☐ _____   ☐ _____   ☐ _____

Concentration / Focus:

NO ABILITY TO FOCUS   1   2   3   4   5   6   7   8   9   10   VERY FOCUSED

SOCIAL ENGAGEMENT	
Who did I see today?	How did I feel in their company?

☐ I preferred to be alone today

List three goals you have for the next year. How would you feel if you accomplished them?

DAILY TRACKER

Today's Date: _____

Went to sleep at: _____   Woke up at: _____   Total hours slept: _____

MOOD / FEELINGS TRACKER			
	Start of Day	Middle of Day	End of Day
Notes			

TRIGGER TRACKER			
Time	Trigger	How did I respond?	What did I feel?

Physical Symptoms:

☐ ENERGIZED	☐ ACHY	☐ RELAXED
☐ TIRED	☐ SLUGGISH	☐ WELL-RESTED
☐ REFRESHED	☐ FATIGUED	☐ JITTERY
☐ WEAK	☐ NUMB	☐ STRONG
☐ _____	☐ _____	☐ _____

Concentration / Focus:

NO ABILITY TO FOCUS   1   2   3   4   5   6   7   8   9   10   VERY FOCUSED

SOCIAL ENGAGEMENT	
Who did I see today?	How did I feel in their company?

☐ I preferred to be alone today

HEALTHY HABIT

Get lost in a good book. Schedule reading time into your routine, even if it is only 10 minutes a day. When we read, we tend to get swept up in the story and forget about our own worries and stress. There is also the added benefit of the accomplishment we feel when we finish reading a book.

DAILY TRACKER

Today's Date: _____

Went to sleep at: _____ Woke up at: _____ Total hours slept: _____

MOOD / FEELINGS TRACKER			
	Start of Day	Middle of Day	End of Day
Notes			

TRIGGER TRACKER			
Time	Trigger	How did I respond?	What did I feel?

Physical Symptoms:

☐ ENERGIZED	☐ ACHY	☐ RELAXED
☐ TIRED	☐ SLUGGISH	☐ WELL-RESTED
☐ REFRESHED	☐ FATIGUED	☐ JITTERY
☐ WEAK	☐ NUMB	☐ STRONG
☐ _____	☐ _____	☐ _____

Concentration / Focus:

NO ABILITY TO FOCUS 1 2 3 4 5 6 7 8 9 10 VERY FOCUSED

SOCIAL ENGAGEMENT	
Who did I see today?	How did I feel in their company?

☐ I preferred to be alone today

What do you feel you take for granted? How could you express more gratitude for these things?

DAILY TRACKER

Today's Date: ....

Went to sleep at: .... Woke up at: .... Total hours slept: ....

MOOD / FEELINGS TRACKER			
	Start of Day	Middle of Day	End of Day
Notes			

TRIGGER TRACKER			
Time	Trigger	How did I respond?	What did I feel?

Physical Symptoms:

☐ ENERGIZED   ☐ ACHY   ☐ RELAXED
☐ TIRED   ☐ SLUGGISH   ☐ WELL-RESTED
☐ REFRESHED   ☐ FATIGUED   ☐ JITTERY
☐ WEAK   ☐ NUMB   ☐ STRONG
☐ ....   ☐ ....   ☐ ....

Concentration / Focus:

NO ABILITY TO FOCUS |—1——2——3——4——5——6——7——8——9——10—| VERY FOCUSED

SOCIAL ENGAGEMENT	
Who did I see today?	How did I feel in their company?

☐ I preferred to be alone today

What is something you are feeling challenged by? How might you begin to work through it?

DAILY TRACKER

Today's Date: _____

Went to sleep at: _____ Woke up at: _____ Total hours slept: _____

MOOD / FEELINGS TRACKER			
	Start of Day	Middle of Day	End of Day
Notes			

TRIGGER TRACKER			
Time	Trigger	How did I respond?	What did I feel?

Physical Symptoms:

- ☐ ENERGIZED
- ☐ TIRED
- ☐ REFRESHED
- ☐ WEAK
- ☐ _____

- ☐ ACHY
- ☐ SLUGGISH
- ☐ FATIGUED
- ☐ NUMB
- ☐ _____

- ☐ RELAXED
- ☐ WELL-RESTED
- ☐ JITTERY
- ☐ STRONG
- ☐ _____

Concentration / Focus:

NO ABILITY TO FOCUS   1   2   3   4   5   6   7   8   9   10   VERY FOCUSED

SOCIAL ENGAGEMENT	
Who did I see today?	How did I feel in their company?

☐ I preferred to be alone today

How have you been unkind to yourself? What can you learn from this behavior?

DAILY TRACKER

Today's Date: _____

Went to sleep at: _____   Woke up at: _____   Total hours slept: _____

MOOD / FEELINGS TRACKER			
	Start of Day	Middle of Day	End of Day
Notes			

TRIGGER TRACKER			
Time	Trigger	How did I respond?	What did I feel?

Physical Symptoms:

- ☐ ENERGIZED
- ☐ TIRED
- ☐ REFRESHED
- ☐ WEAK
- ☐ _____

- ☐ ACHY
- ☐ SLUGGISH
- ☐ FATIGUED
- ☐ NUMB
- ☐ _____

- ☐ RELAXED
- ☐ WELL-RESTED
- ☐ JITTERY
- ☐ STRONG
- ☐ _____

Concentration / Focus:

NO ABILITY TO FOCUS   1   2   3   4   5   6   7   8   9   10   VERY FOCUSED

SOCIAL ENGAGEMENT	
Who did I see today?	How did I feel in their company?

☐ I preferred to be alone today

What have you learned about yourself through your experience with depression?

DAILY TRACKER

Today's Date: _____

Went to sleep at: _____ Woke up at: _____ Total hours slept: _____

MOOD / FEELINGS TRACKER			
	Start of Day	Middle of Day	End of Day
Notes			

TRIGGER TRACKER			
Time	Trigger	How did I respond?	What did I feel?

Physical Symptoms:

☐ ENERGIZED ☐ ACHY ☐ RELAXED
☐ TIRED ☐ SLUGGISH ☐ WELL-RESTED
☐ REFRESHED ☐ FATIGUED ☐ JITTERY
☐ WEAK ☐ NUMB ☐ STRONG
☐ _____ ☐ _____ ☐ _____

Concentration / Focus:

NO ABILITY TO FOCUS 1 2 3 4 5 6 7 8 9 10 VERY FOCUSED

SOCIAL ENGAGEMENT	
Who did I see today?	How did I feel in their company?

☐ I preferred to be alone today

HEALTHY HABIT

Cultivate a growth mindset rather than a fixed mindset. Those with a growth mindset are willing to take risks and make mistakes, see their perceived failures as opportunities to grow, and are open to receiving feedback. Take time to evaluate where in your life you can incorporate more of a growth mindset. For example, what can you do that is out of your comfort zone, and how can you use it as an opportunity to move yourself forward and learn from it?

RESOURCES

National Suicide Prevention Lifeline. This service is available 24/7 at 1-800-273-TALK (8255) and offers free and confidential support for anyone experiencing suicidal thoughts or suicidal ideation.

Hoffman Institute provides an extensive list of words to use when describing your feelings.
HoffmanInstitute.org/wp-content/uploads/Practices-Feelings Sensations.pdf.

Insight Timer is a free meditation app and website that helps with stress, anxiety, and sleep. They even provide virtual yoga classes and live events.
InsightTimer.com

Psychology Today is a great website with a database of therapist, psychologist, and psychiatrist profiles. You can search by your city or zip code.
PsychologyToday.com

Therapist Aid provides free worksheets and interactive tools to help with your mental and general well-being. You can search by topic or content type.
TherapistAid.com

HelpGuide is a free resource that provides content about mental health. You can find meditations and articles organized by category and topic.
HelpGuide.org

The Universe Talks will send daily reminders and inspiration to your inbox to uplift and empower you.
TUT.com

Calm is a meditation app that offers various guided meditations to help improve sleep, reduce stress, improve focus, and aid general self-improvement.
Get.Calm.com

REFERENCES

"Box Breathing: Getting Started with Box Breathing, How to Do It, Benefits and Tips." WebMD. Accessed October 27, 2021. WebMD.com /balance/what-is-box-breathing.

Cunha, Lúzie Fofonka, Lucia Campos Pellanda, and Caroline Tozzi Reppold. "Positive Psychology and Gratitude Interventions: A Randomized Clinical Trial." *Frontiers in Psychology* (2019). DOI.org/10.3389 /fpsyg.2019.00584.

"Depression." World Health Organization. Accessed September 22, 2021. WHO.int/news-room/fact-sheets/detail/depression.

"Easy Habits That Can Improve Your Mental Health." WebMD. Accessed October 27, 2021. WebMD.com/depression/ss/slideshow-easy -habits-improve-mental-health.

"Exercise Is an All-Natural Treatment to Fight Depression." Harvard Health, February 2, 2021. Health.Harvard.edu/mind-and-mood /exercise-is-an-all-natural-treatment-to-fight-depression.

Hofmann, Stefan G., and Angelina F. Gómez. "Mindfulness-Based Interventions for Anxiety and Depression." *Psychiatric Clinics of North America* 40, no. 4 (December 2017): 739–749. DOI.org/10.1016/j .psc.2017.08.008.

Krpan, Katherine M., Ethan Kross, Marc G. Berman, Patricia J. Deldin, Mary K. Askren, and John Jonides. "An Everyday Activity as a Treatment for Depression: The Benefits of Expressive Writing for People Diagnosed with Major Depressive Disorder." *Journal of Affective Disorders* 150, no. 3 (September 25, 2013): 1148–1151. DOI.org/10.1016/j. jad.2013.05.065.

LePera, Nicole. *How to Do the Work: Recognize Your Patterns, Heal from Your Past, and Create Your Self.* New York: Harper Wave, 2021.

Ljungberg, Tina, Emma Bondza, and Connie Lethin. "Evidence of the Importance of Dietary Habits Regarding Depressive Symptoms and Depression." *International Journal of Environmental Research and Public Health* 17, no. 5 (March 2020): 1616. DOI.org/10.3390/ijerph17051616.

"Major Depression." National Institute of Mental Health. U.S. Department of Health and Human Services. Accessed September 15, 2021. NIMH.nih.gov/health/statistics/major-depression.

Merrimack Valley Psychological Associates. "Healthy Habits to Cope with Depression." Accessed July 20, 2021. MVPsych.com/blog/habits-for-depression.

Saeed, Sy Atezaz, Karlene Cunningham, and Richard M. Bloch. "Depression and Anxiety Disorders: Benefits of Exercise, Yoga, and Meditation." *American Family Physician* 99, no. 10 (May 15, 2019): 620–627. AAFP.org/afp/2019/0515/p620.html.

Van der Kolk, Bessel. *The Body Keeps the Score: Brain, Mind, and Body in the Healing of Trauma.* New York: Penguin Books, 2015.

"What Is Depression?" American Psychiatric Association. Accessed October 27, 2021. Psychiatry.org/patients-families/depression/what-is-depression.

Acknowledgments

This book was a true gift and honor to write. A huge thank-you to Kayla Park for your guidance and for answering all my questions along the way. A special thank-you to Marcel for your support, patience, and love. None of this would have been possible without my family and friends who always show up. And I could never have done this without my favorite four-legged writing companion, Charlie.

About the Author

Missy Beck, MA, LMF T, is a licensed psychotherapist and mindset coach based in Los Angeles, California. She has worked in the mental health field for more than 10 years with clients who experience depression, anxiety, relationship struggles, trauma, addiction, loss, and grief. She is trained in EMDR and mindfulness and is a 200-hour registered yoga teacher. In addition, she is passionate about psychedelics and their power to heal and offers ketamine-assisted psychotherapy. Beck blends traditional psychology with mindful awareness to bring together the mind, body, and spirit. She can be found at MissyBeck.com and on Instagram @iammissybeck.